pamphlet Architecture

ARCHITECTURE AS A TRANSLATION OF MUSIC

edited by Elizabeth Martin

princeton Architectural press

In Memoriam
John Cage 1912–1992

I corresponded with John Cage informally about music + architecture. He was a magnet for interesting inquiry and always gave fascinating, often loaded responses, which have become part of the concluding notes of *PA 16*.

Princeton Architectural Press
37 East 7th Street
New York, New York 10003
212.995.9620

Editor: Elizabeth Martin
Design and Frontispiece: David Hadlock
Cover: Marcos Novak, Elizabeth Martin, and David Hadlock
Copy Editors: Sabrina Silver, John Martin, and Hadley Soutter
Publisher: Kevin C. Lippert
Editorial Assistant: Heidi Liebes
Production Assistants: Jane Alexander, David Bliss

I gratefully acknowledge the generous support of the Jerome Chazen
Foundation and Mary Bernadette Martin.

Library of Congress Cataloging-in-Publication Data
Architecture as a translation of music / edited by Elizabeth Martin.
        p. cm. — (Pamphlet architecture ; 16)
    Includes bibliographical references.
    ISBN 1-56898-012-4
    1. Architecture—Research. 2. Architecture—Philosophy.
3. Music and architecture. I. Martin, Elizabeth, 1962– .
II. Series: Pamphlet architecture ; no. 16.
    NA2005.A67 1994
    720' . 1'04—dc20
                                                    94-22892
                                                         CIP

Pamphlet Architecture was initiated in 1977 as an independent vehicle to
criticize, question, and exchange views. Each issue is assembled by an
individual author/architect. For information, pamphlet proposals, or
contributions, please write to: Pamphlet Architecture, c/o Princeton Archi
tectural Press, 37 E. 7th Street, New York, NY 10003.

Pamphlets published:

*Available only in the collection *Pamphlet Architecture 1-10*

CONTENTS

My high school writing teacher, Mr. Springbored,* taught our class that there are four distinct categories of writing: informative, descriptive, analytical, and entertaining. Attempting to fulfill an assignment, I produced what I thought was a strictly informative paper on "Maintaining a Sea Monkey Farm in Your Own Home." After reading it to the class, I was told it wasn't informative; it was entertaining. As clear as the four categories seemed, too many lines crossed between them, blurring their distinction. This has led me to recognize that the world is not so neatly confined and defined as I was always taught.

So, rather than relying on a confined, separated definition of music and architecture to introduce *PA16*, I've fallen back to the root of each art: the eye and the ear. The eye and the ear resemble each other in construction, number, and in the function of their parts resulting in the obvious perception of analogous properties of matter. The eye lends itself to a visual field; the ear to an aural field. Architecture represents the art of design in space; music, the art of design in time. Nature continually manifests motion in space or motion and space bound together as one;

it is LIFE. The properties of space and time are inseparable. Without time and space, matter is inconceivable; it is a dead thing. Space gives form and proportion; time supplies it with life and measure.

This study of music + architecture is a work in progress rather than a definitive and exhaustive study of architecture as a translation of music. I am assembling this study to stimulate criticism and discussion of the basic issues and perhaps involve other investigators in the task of extending this sketch to the creative process. The ten musicians and architects whose work provides the basic material for this study explore the language, philosophy and character of music + architecture. Their work successfully breaks down the culturally erected barriers that separate the music audience from the architecture audience. Here a new stage is being built; the old idea of music + architecture isn't erased, but it is out of focus, blurred, and unsharpened.

The pamphlet is divided into four sections: Vitruvius Program, y– Condition, Case Studies, and Concluding Notes. The Case Studies are further divided into three point of views: Based on Acoustics, Instrument as Architec-

ture, and Layered Relationships. These three approaches are not the hard and fast categories that Mr. Springbored implied, but are instead offered here as other means of exploration. Overtones from one approach often sound into another, making no one project a pure representation of a single point of view. For example, Michael Brewster's Geneva By-Pass project explores the acoustics of three consecutive tunnels, but also shares the qualities of a wind instrument.

We live in a culture that readily and pervasively privileges the eye over the ear. I have assembled *PA16* to counterbalance this unconscious tendency and to spark an interest in the translation between the two mediums of music and architecture. By tying together the adjacencies and overhearing the varied mutations of visual sound and acoustical space imagined and installed, I hope this pamphlet will give another sense to the numerous ways music and architecture have mutated and cross-fertilized one another.

"If you put something inside that space you can see the music. It's a cool idea—why aren't you doing it?"(Luke)*

vitruvius program

The Vitruvius Program is an educational organization devoted to the development of teaching materials and methods in the field of architecture. Vitruvius was founded by Kathleen and Eugene Kupper under the auspices of the Southern California Institute of Architecture and is named after an architect who wrote the *Ten Books of Architecture*, the oldest and most influential work on architecture in existence. The very first words of this text are devoted to the *"Education of the Architect."* We understand from Vitruvius that architecture is not a specialized and exclusive subject, but one of the most universal and inclusive of human abilities. Learning architecture is a creative integration of doing and knowing and the importance of each in solving problems. These are abilities that our children can develop, that will act as the foundation for their growth and understanding of the world with an open mind.

A five-week workshop on music and architecture was developed to explore spatial ideas of sound, noise, acoustics, melody, and harmony as well as construction techniques found in the design of musical instruments. The students work in a studio environment that functions as a laboratory for developing projects, ideas, and curriculums in design. The workshop began by reading Claude Clement's *The Voice of the Wood*, which is a story about an Italian violin maker who carves a violin that captures the transforming powers of music and "only a heart in tune with the voice of the wood can draw a sound from the instrument." With a program of a violin-makers shop, drawings and models capturing the experience of the instrument-maker's craft were created. Violin-making is a discipline and as such it offers the potential for the pursuit of a way of life, unique to each individual, but tied to a lifelong dedication to a craft that demands constant refinement. Fusing the objective, as well as the intuitive, responses, an attempt was made to weave the poetic interpretation of

11

"The Architect should be equipped with the knowledge of many branches of study and varied kinds of learning, for in the architectural judgement all of the work of other arts is brought into test...therefore let our architect be educated, skillful with the pencil, instructed in geometry, knowledgeable in history, follow the philosophers with attention, understand music...and many kinds of learning, I think that no one has the right to proclaim oneself as architect hastily.... Those, therefore, who from tender years receive instruction in the various forms of learning, recognize the same stamp on all the arts, and an integration of all fields of study, so that they can more readily comprehend them all."
Marcus Vitruvius Pollio

the craftsman's ideologies into the material fabric of a building. The process of design was informed by the nature of the act itself.

Drawings and models were created while viewing the Music Animation Machine, which is video-illustrating computer software developed by Stephen Malinoswki. Like a conventional music score, the software contains information about pitch, timing, and instrumentation in traditional musical notation that can be grasped without musical training. It is simply an animated, graphical music score for listeners and viewers. The drawings were created over two sessions, layering watercolor shapes over penciled forms over ink musical patterns. The models were made from bar-blocks by utilizing techniques of layering with an additive assembly of architectonic components that were influenced by the musical material of the Music Animation Machine. This computer program gave a wonderful insight into the architecture of sound.

The workshop continued by building hybrid instruments and creating notation systems that became inventions of their own. It was as if they developed a new language by developing a simple system of writing down music and using it to play the music they composed on their hybrid instruments (shown on the right). The symbols and instructions on a score tells the musician which notes to play, what rhythm to follow, how loud or soft, and how fast or slow. It became a way of communicating, describing, narrating, and exchanging their ideas by first translating sounds into images then into a notation system. The students' projects examined the movement of language from what they understood to what they created. The children decided that they didn't really like music, but liked noise. Instead of creating musical notation, they began to draw noise patterns. Music is a form of sound and is carried through the air to our ears by sound waves. The students explored sound waves by building a room that a bat inhabits. Bats have poor eyesight, but a very good sense of hearing. They can hear ultrasound—high-pitched sounds that are way beyond the human hearing range. Bats can use ultrasound to find their way around. When a bat makes a high-

"Criss-cross sound waves are the flight patterns of the bat inside." (Nora)*

"This box represents a whole-tone but don't tell anyone because I'm gonna make this a famous idea through my secret agent. He'd be here but he's on a special mission now." (Mitchell)*

pitched squeak, the sound bounces off the wall of the cave and returns to the bat as an ultrasound echo. From the amount of time between the squeak and the echo, a bat can tell the distance to the wall.

Through these kind of studios or workshops, young people develop a sense of imagination and relevance in addressing constructive decisions and designs for physical and social systems. Artistic and problem-solving activities in all media are explored as an intellectual and creative discipline. It's as important to learn how to design, draw, and think spatially as it is to learn how to read. The Vitruvius Program's purpose is not to teach children to be architects but to build self-esteem and encourage problem solving by using architecture as a tool.

Vitruvius listed music as one of the "essentials" of architecture, used primarily to "tune ballistae, catapultae, and scorpiones to the proper key."

Workshop teachers: Annie Coggan, Liz Martin; preparation of curriculum: Liz Martin; saxophone and guitar demonstration: Mark Baez.

Books: Taber, Anthony. *The Boy Who Stopped Time.* New York: McElberry Books, 1993.
Clement, Claude. *The Voice of the Wood.* Translated by Lenny Holt. New York: Dial Books,1988.
Rosen, Michael, editor. "Ears, Eyes, Legs and Arms," *South and North, East and West.* Massachusetts: Candlewick Press, 1992, pp. 50-52.

"When I pull the string tighter it sounds different." (Robin)*

"When I look through it I can see the other side of my instrument but when I blow, it echoes! Does that mean I'm hearing the other side?" (Elizabeth)*

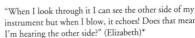

vitruvius program

"Can I play my painting next week?" (Matthew)   "Layer Smayer, so what?" (Luke)   "This is a frozen kind of music engine." (Luke)*

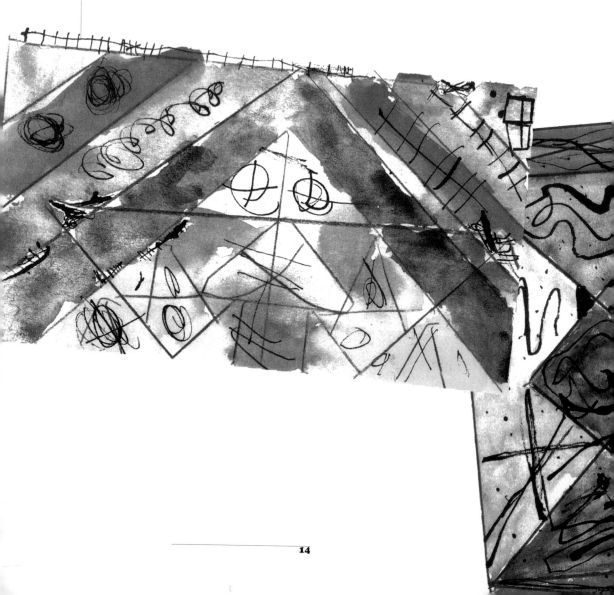

* all captions are quotes from the children during the workshop.

vitruvius program

y— CONDITION

E

L

I

Z

A

B

E

T

H

M

A

R

T

I

N

Let's say, simply for a point of departure, that there exists a definable membrane through which meaning can move when translating from one discipline to another. [What I mean by membrane is a thin, pliable layer that connects two things and is, in this case, the middle position of music + architecture.] The membrane is similar perhaps to the role of a semi-tone or semi-vowel in the study of phonetics. A semi-tone is a transitional sound heard during articulation linking two phonemically contiguous sounds, like the *y* sound often heard between the *i* and the *e* of quiet. I am suggesting that something similar occurs, a *y*– condition, in the middle position of music + architecture when translating one to the other. Louis Kahn once described great architecture as that which starts with the immeasurable, proceeds through the measurable, and returns to the immeasurable. He was describing a process by which the spark of genius in an idea is carried by way of investigation, drawing, and construction into a finished piece of architecture. In this case, starting at the immeasurable is beginning to explore the *y*– condition of music + architecture. Although music + architecture have different phenomenal presences, the underlying organization of their respective formal structures and colloquialisms are similar. The aim of this investigation is to explore as a DESIGN TOOL the idea of translation defined as a "rendering of the same ideas in a different language from the original." This is accomplished by searching for a methodology that may lead to a means of expression for the *y*– condition of music + architecture. The *y*– condition explores the two art forms in a comparative way, as far as necessary limits will allow, and through experimentation discovers that there exists between them a consistent and organic union. A relationship starts in the physical laws of light and optics on the one hand, and sound and hearing on the other. In their rudimentary media of expression, such as notes, meters, tones and lines, colors and geometrical forms, the union is carried on by their respective systems of artistic and imaginative composition, design and execution.

program The focus of the *y*– condition project was to create and define a methodology. Because the exploration in itself was more important than the specifics of any one program, I chose a program and site that exist only in theory. I searched for a program that by its very nature is resonant with theories of minimal music. The program is based on the idea of a center in which a synthesis of the entire field of knowledge can occur— a super-tech earth station—a center that Lebbeus Woods invented and called an Epicyclarium. It is a structure composed of the forms and spaces that house the instruments of an advanced electronics technology

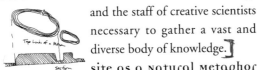

and the staff of creative scientists necessary to gather a vast and diverse body of knowledge.

site as a natural metaphor I discovered that a particular land formation, a mesa, illustrates characteristics of minimal music: simplicity, repetition, illusion/perception, events, phase-shifting, complexity and sudden alterations of density.

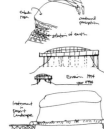

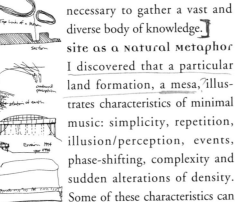

Some of these characteristics can be recognized by viewing the mesa physically while others become apparent by analyzing topographical maps/geo-notation systems. Using a mesa as a natural metaphor serves as an abstract interpretation of the interplay of different but related elements.

music composition and theory I started this project by analyzing several scores of music to discover the essences of the works, specifically those of minimal classical composers: Steven Reich, Terry Rily, Philip Glass, and La Monte Young. I chose to study contemporary classical music to implicitly challenge the appropriateness of certain traditions in architectural form-making, such as the idea of utility and purposive form. In minimal and traditional classical music, the basic palate of ideas and raw materials are the same; but in minimal music some of the rules of traditional classical music are either broken, lost, or exploited. From this analysis, I outlined the basic ideology of minimal music, pointing out why, with the same ingredients, it is different from traditional classical music. Minimal music is the extreme reduction of musical means in terms of harmony, counterpoint, and theory of form. According to Arnold Schönberg, the doctrine of musical composition is usually divided into these three areas: **Harmony** is the doctrine of chords and their possible connections with regard to their tectonic, melodic, and rhythmic values and relative weights. **counterpoint** is the doctrine of the movement of voices with regard to motivic combination. **theory of form** deals with disposition for the construction and development of musical thoughts.

y— CONDITION

E
L
I
Z
A
B
E
T
H

M
A
R
T
I
N

To achieve this, a minimalist considers only the essential factors of his/her perceptions and discards the rest. Minimal music is composed in such a way as to deny hierarchic structure and patterning resulting in a succession of events rather than a progression of events.

Traditional music is linear, having a beginning and an end similar to those of a classical novel, where the denouement resolves the conflict of the plot. Minimal music creates a cyclical experience much like that of a factory: repetition of a product being made.

Minimal music focuses on repetitive cycles where the basic form is repeated and where smaller units with different rhythms are added like a wheel-work. Minimal music discards the traditional harmonic schemes of tension and relaxation and the musical narrative that goes with them. Traditional music uses ideas of repetition to tell a story. In Maurice Ravel's *Bolero*, for example, an eight-measure theme is repeated over and over, building up to a climax as in the story of the bullfight it is telling.

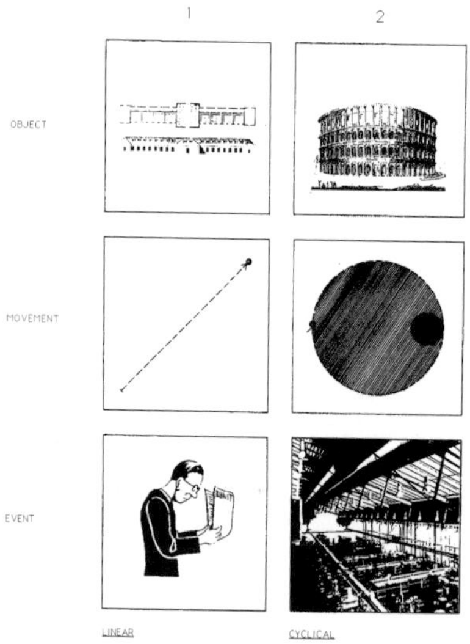

OBJECT

MOVEMENT

EVENT

LINEAR   CYCLICAL

LINEAR—CYCLICAL

1. CREATES CYCLES OF EVENTS RATHER THAN A LINEAR SEQUENCE. A LINEAR SEQUENCE IS END-ORIENTED, SIMILAR TO A TRADITIONAL CLASSIC NOVEL WHERE THE DENOUEMENT RESOLVES THE CONFLICT OF THE PLOT.
CYCLE OF EVENTS IS MUCH LIKE A PRODUCT BEING MADE IN A FACTORY.

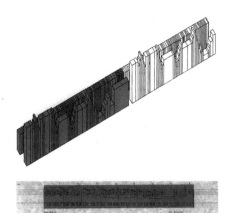

TRADITIONAL REPETITION

II. FOCUSES ON MUSICAL COMPONENTS LIKE RHYTHM, MELODY, AND HARMONY. PRE-FIGURED BY UNDERLYING DRAMA-TIZED CONSTRUCTION, SYMBOLIZATION OF SITUATIONS, LIMITATION OF ACTION.

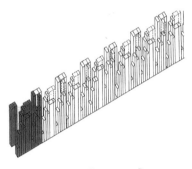

MINIMAL REPETITION

III. CREATES A FEELING OF MOVEMENT. THE PULSE PULLS ATTENTION AWAY FROM THE DETAILS OF THE FORM TO THE OVER-ALL PROCESS. THE PIECE OF MUSIC IS LITER-ALLY THE PROCESS.

OBJECT—SPACE RELATIONSHIP

IV. SUDDEN ALTERATIONS OF DENSITY. ONE MODULAR FIGURE IS STRETCHED AND CONTRACTED OVER A CONSTANT PATTERN OF SOUND MATERIAL.

Y—CONDITION

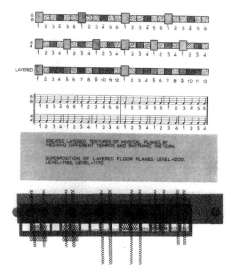

v. CREATES LAYERED TEXTURES OF MUSICAL PLANES BY MESHING DIFFERENT TEMPOS AND RHYTHMIC PATTERNS. PENETRATES THE INNER ESSENCE OF SOUND BY BRINGING OUT THE SIMPLICITY AND COMPLEXITY.

vi. FOCUSES ON REPETITIVE CYCLES WHERE THE BASIC FORM IS REPEATED AND PHASE-SHIFTED. THIS IS A DEVICE USED WHERE A FIXED PART REPEATS THE BASIC PATTERN THROUGHOUT THE PIECE WHILE THE SECOND PARTS ACCELERATE TO TAKE IT OUT OF PHASE.

Graphic Music *exercise,*

I composed a piece of graphic music to visually communicate minimal music theory. The piece is graphically based on the sets and ordering procedures in minimal music. This exercise diagrams the non-narrative and non-teleological process.

In the graphically composed music drawing, one square equals one eighth note, within a range of forty-five notes and a pattern of duration; symbols were assigned to various modes of articulation and a simple set of rhythmic cells were created, connected by lines of chord members and successive notes at the same dynamic level to complete the structure.

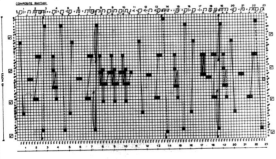

As an additional exercise, I developed a building in the exact process. One square equals the smallest unit—a beam, wall, or floor plane—within a range of forty-five units and a pattern of duration; symbols (a1, a2, a3 and b1, b2, b3) were assigned to various modes of articulation and a simple set of spatial units were shown stretched and compressed in time and then connected by lines of relationships with the same spatial quality to complete the structure. This layered drawing became the framework for the creation of the *y*– condition.

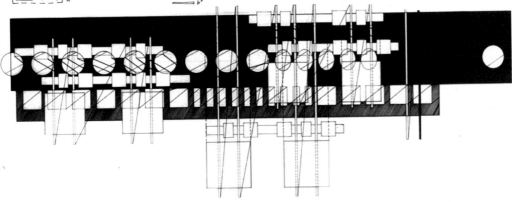

Y- CONDITION

cycle of events In minimal music, tempos and rhythmic patterns are meshed together, creating layered planes. At certain points all lines in the piece emphasizing their first beat of a particular measure interlock, creating a cycle of events. In common usage, an event is something that occurs at a certain place at a certain time. We can think of space and time as being composed of events. In the $y-$ condition, an event is the conflux of a phase shift. Specifically, a cycle of events is the coincidental meetings of the different phases at their point of interlock following a mathematical system that determines its spatial position.

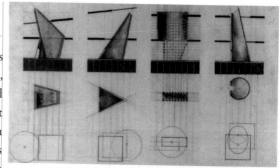

Photo/Benny Chan

phase-shifted space

For the cycle of events that occur in the Epicyclarium, the phase-shifted space determines the form. In the phase shift, a fixed part repeats the basic pattern throughout a piece while the second part accelerates to take it out of phase. This produces an ever-changing alignment against the first part and results in the stressing of constantly different notes.

Phase-shifted space is multi-dimensional space; it's coordinates no longer represent a place, but rather an event. As a series of events travels through time, it carves out a specific portrait; through phase-shifted space that portrait is mutated. In this particular case, the first plane remains a constant while the second and third planes are shifted slightly. The form occurring within the punctures is determined by the planes above and below it. In both minimal music theory and $y-$ condition, a phase shift creates a behavioral portrait of events in time.

Alteration of density Another characteristic of minimal music is that it is structured to create a feeling of movement. Due to a sudden alteration of density, one modular figure is added or subtracted from itself and layered over a constant pattern of sound material. The result is a number of rising and falling composite figures that are stretched and compressed, creating a restricted or extended time-sense.

Cubic elements of the Epicyclarium move along a
mechanical track, which is divided
into 365 increments. This
movement represents the
cycle of the year. The
largest space between the
moving cubes and the stat-
ic structure is an observation deck at
the summer solstice; the smallest is a
corridor or passageway at the winter
solstice. The movement of the structures creates an ever-changing spa-
tial relationship in a rhythmic-arithmetic manner,
resulting in an alteration of density.

Summer

Winter

Photo/Benny Chan

Photo/Benny Chan

Transformation of Dimension In our own bodies
physical hearing can be thought of as a dialogue
between the inside and outside. In much the same way,
architecture also resembles a dialogue connecting outside and inside; specifically, the facade can be thought
of as the meeting place of internal and external space.
In the 1930s, many architects used a mathematical pattern of measurement analysis to develop proportion
systems; Jan Hoogstand's work is an example. The
facade uses the mathematical pattern of
dimension analysis and the physically calcu-
lable behavior of light and its reflection, both
of which aid in translating a subjective image
into architecture. It's an attempt at using a
spatial grammar as a $y-$ condition instead of a
direct comparable system of proportion in
reference to the notes in music.
INTERNAL SPACE is determined by the column centers of the supporting structures,

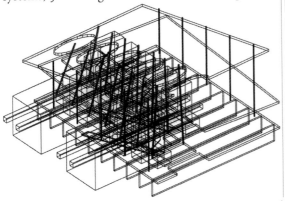

Y – CONDITION

23

floor to floor access, and an average clerestory height, resulting in a proportion of 2:40:16. EXTERNAL SPACE is the average column bay, average width of building, and an average of the facade height, resulting in a proportion of 28:80:33. From this dimension analysis, the following series was established in related figures: 14:40:16; this determined the facade. Setting up a series of relationships similar to this is the seed that begins a composition in minimal music and therefore is incorporated into the design process.

Repetition as a form of Discovery The $y-$ condition creates things removed from their conventional architectural or musical representation. Its sequences do not lie in an accurate translation of our external awareness, but in the internal logic these sequences display. The Epicyclarium, one possible manifestation of the $y-$ condition, describes complex relationships between objects and events, between space and its purpose, between time and distance, between visual and aural, between movement and object. The process of exploration of the $y-$ condition leads to a discovery that can only be be seen against the backdrop of another discovery and another and another and another.

"Whenever a thought presents itself as a commonly accepted truth, and we take the trouble to develop it, we will find that it is a discovery." Lautremont, *Poesies*.

I would like to thank the faculty of SCI-Arc, especially Neil Denari, for their input and for their generous assistance: John Klingman, Carol Lowry, Alexander Baseman Kichen, Bill Hogan, Sara Warshaw, Jim Bassett, Evan Mulho, and Spencer Hunt.

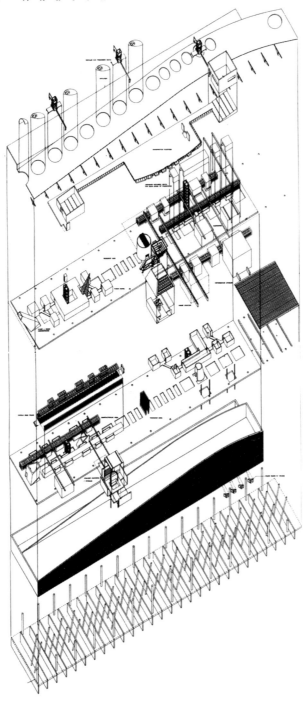

Y— CONDITION

case studies———————————————

Based on acoustics

acoustic [Gr. *akoustos*, heard, from *akouein*, to hear] pertaining to the ears, to the sense of hearing, or to the doctrine of sounds.

The following acoustically based projects use sound as a raw material. Each pursues connections that interact and combine, in order to fill spaces with the simultaneous attraction of the architectural and the sonorous. The power of acoustics has its roots in the way that it ties a person into the sound of a room. We ourselves make the room resound with our steps or speech, or by simply breathing. This interconnection between humans and space is a dialogue that enables us to experience ourselves in the sound of the room. We have the ability to create and recreate any sound with precise accuracy in time, and to shift it or move it around in space with the same precision. We can use sound as a building material for spatial design along with light, shadow, or concrete. These projects work within spaces that are less assisted by the eye than the ear, heightening our acoustical awareness of the space. By minimizing our relationship to the visual, we focus our attention on the aural. As a result, our perception of sound becomes more space oriented.

L E I T N E R

A M A C H E R

B R E W S T E R

LE CYLINDRE SONORE

Sunk into a bamboo-filled, valley-like landscape of the Parc de la Villette, Le Cylindre Sonore was created as a publicly funded intervention artistique for Section 4 of the park. The double cylinder, the top of which is on grade bordered by the tree-lined streets, is an integral part of the park's promenade. Before entering the bamboo garden, one descends into the sound space, and coming from the garden, one enters the sound space before climbing the steps back up the park. Although constructed as a static, platonic solid inserted into the landscape, it was conceived and built as an event in time, a sequence of experiences with a beginning and an end. As an acoustical container, its spatial boundaries have relevance only as they unfold, transform, or superimpose the experience of sound.

The inside diameter of the double cylinder is ten meters; its height, five meters. Behind each of the eight perforated, precast concrete panels (each measuring 1.2 x 3.7 meters) that compose the inner cylinder are three speakers mounted at different heights. The voids between the eight panels act as columns through which sound is composed and elaborated. The space between the two cylinders, besides acting as a service corridor with access to the underground control room, serves as a resonator. Eight narrow vertical strips of water are acoustical fine-tuning devices, further refining the conditions under which the sensorium of the ears, skin, and brain functions. Emanating sounds attract the curious, inviting them to stop, to listen attentively, and to linger; sonorously and spatially, thought and senses are bound within and liberated from this place.

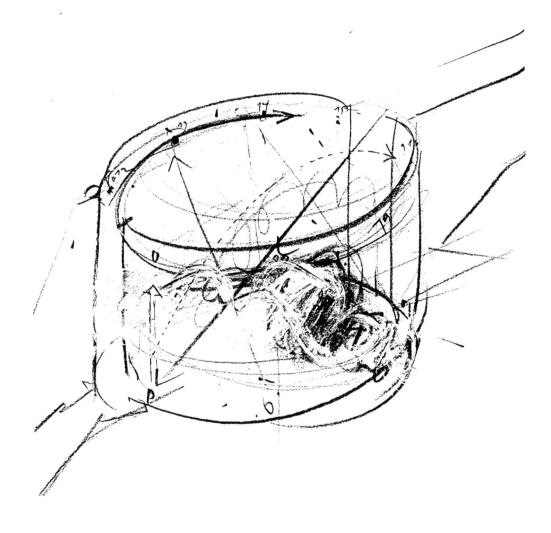

LE CYLINDRE SONORE

B
E
R
N
H
A
R
D

L
E
I
T
N
E
R

The combined effect is the acoustical delineation of space and the physical massing of sound. Sound is no longer exclusively the instrument of musical expression; designed with precision, it becomes a building material in the creation of space. Sound's ability to merge with other sounds and its lack of borders represent a phenomenal equivalent to the artistic concepts of interpenetration, nonobjectiveness, and nonobstruction. Active processes that use sound's invisibility and temporality interpret sound as having a characteristic of nonbeing. By enclosing a moment, Le Cylindre Sonore creates a field in which acoustical experience may occur using what Artur Schnabel calls "kompositionsprozesse"; he states: "It is not the aural effect that is prescribed, but the process that generates it." In this instance, product and process are the same; there is no longer a question of the reproduction of an experience—each visit to the cylinder

produces the work for the first time. John Cage wrote that the music of the past was "dealing with conceptions and their communication, but the new music being created has nothing to do with the communication of concept, only to do with perception." Le Cylindre Sonore attempts the architectural equivalent—to free space from the burden of representation and to offer it instead as a purely perceptual dimension.

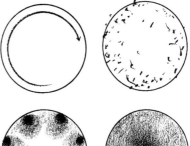

LE CYLINDRE SONORE

Facing Page:

Top: Illustration of hearing within a human ear. Bottom: Curved portion of
Synaptic Island installation space (labeled X on plan of space).

SYNAPTIC ISLAND:
A PSYBERTONAL TOPOLOGY

M
A
R
Y
A
N
N
E
A
M
A
C
H
E
R

The multi-media work, Synaptic Island: A Psybertonal Topology, is staged architecturally as a dramatic narrative, evolving throughout the space and joining both indoor and outdoor spaces of the Tokushima 21st Century Cultural Information Center during CyberSound Week (30 April–5 May 1992). The Information Center is part of the Tokushima Bunka-no-Mori Park, which consists of five pavilions including a library and a modern art museum. CyberSound Week explores the relationship between advanced technology and our culture.

Exploring acoustics, perceptual psychology, architecture, and computer technology, Synaptic Island creates a space where the listener becomes the vibrating instrument in a transformed environment. The music is engineered as sound, felt throughout the body, as well as heard. We might naively assume that professional musicians need only to know how to count, recognize, and name notes, tones, and chords, etc., but are not really concerned with describing them physically, to be able to experience what is inside the sounds—what they are as energy—all the complex and interesting events take place within the timbres. The music in Synaptic Island reinforces additional tones consciously and cultivates interplays between tones that originate in the ears, the brain, and the room—this can be thought of as perceptual geography. Perceptual geography seeks ways of composing in which tones, originating within human anatomy, exist in their own right by becoming perceptually more than an accident of acoustic tones in the room, resulting in a conscious interplay between them. Synaptic Island explores the way sound infiltrates the ear and our bodies by using the architectural characteristics of the Information Center to create a dramatic sound experience.

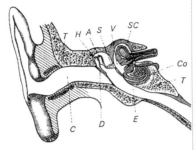

Music is connected to the phenomenal characteristics of sound. The object of perceptual geography is to learn to compose spatial dimensions in music—the kind of aural dimension we experience in life, but usually not in music. The idea is to create a world for the audience to enter where architecture magnifies the expressive dimensions of the music. In this approach, the phrases of the music are choreographed to sound at specific heights and locations. Tactile in presence, they appear both larger than life and small enough to touch, heard as though miles away, or felt inside the listener. Sound is sent through the solid medium of the building before entering the space. These structure-borne sound waves travel faster and create a larger wavelength than airborne sound. The wavelength we feel for an airborne sound-wave for middle C is only four feet; the structure-borne sound wave is over twenty feet. Making use of this discovery, we can control, reinforce, and enhance acoustical shapes to create the music within a specific space. Referring to this work, Marvin Minsky stated that it "explores the ways that subtle environmental changes affect how we see the world from moment to moment."

SYNAPTIC ISLAND: A PSYBERTONAL TOPOLOGY

M
A
R
Y

A

N

N

E

A

M

A

C

H

E

R

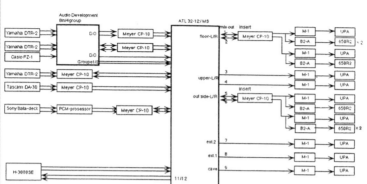

In responding to music, our ears act as instruments, sounding their own tones, in addition to those produced by musical instruments in the room, like another instrument joining the orchestra. Neuroanatomy responds and gives shape to the most subtle traces of acoustical information. We hear tones other than the given acoustical tones taking their shape inside our ears, as the membrane vibrates in response to the given acoustic tones. Think of yourself, as the listener, responding to certain extremely sensitive resonant instruments within the anatomical structure of your own inner ears. The simplest case is demonstrated when two sine waves sound and we respond by creating three more tones in our ears. The source of these sounds is NOT created by an electronic multi-speaker, but by the sounds responding within the space. As a result, another sound system is then created where the building is the speaker and the listener's brain is the mixing board. In this way, not only the building but the participant becomes integral to the experience.

Works in this genre are productions of music and sets that have evolving scenarios that build one upon the other, over a period of several days or weeks. Synaptic Island pushes this idea even further by adopting the mini-series format of television and popular comics, composing a musical narrative "to be continued" in consecutive episodes. The audience walks into "the world of the story" upon entering the set. Complex sound shapes are designed to interact with the architectural structures of the room before reaching the listener; an

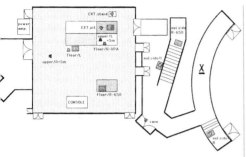

atmosphere that gives a sense of being immersed inside a cinematic close-up, anticipating virtual immersion environments. Places of thematic focus—rooms, corridors, walls, doorways, balconies and stairways—are selected to create the scenes and vary within the story line for each scenario over each performance. They are then staged as installations of music and sets with feature length performances, each having a duration of eighty minutes to one hour and forty minutes.

Listening to and observing sound structures is very much like observing cell structures: looking at "life within" to discover and understand its special features, order of shapes, and unique intelligence before composing new theories or rearrangements. Synaptic Island: A Psybertonal Topology explores the notion of perceptual geography by combining the perceptual dimension in the acoustic space with that of tone sensations originating within the anatomy.

未来から吹き寄せられる江戸の音色
「日墓楽結縁」 高橋悠治(PM1:00~5:00)
三邦演奏「熊済野饗」他一西垣柚子(PM2:00&PM4:00)

極限まで拡大された音響ミクロ圏に
展開する2部構成の音の演劇
"SYNAPTIC ISLAND" A Psybertonal Topology
Music and Sets by Maryanne Amacher
6 performances PM 7:30.
"Headlands Chronicle 1" Apr. 30—May 2
"Neurophonic Exercises": Neura: Swirl
InterAural Gold" May 3—5

[サウンド・ヴァーチャル・リアリティ]
仮想音響空間の6日間
サイバーサウンドウィーク
1992年4月30日[木] 5月5日[火]
会場:徳島県立21世紀館イベントホール

CYBER SOUND WEEK

GENEVA BY-PASS

Along the N 1a Highway, the lush Swiss countryside is broken up by a series of long claustrophobic tunnels. The Geneva By-Pass project is a competition entry that proposes to physically improve and aestheticize the motorist's transit through three subterranean passages by using sound and light to emphasize the kinesthetic experience of travelling.

While their well-designed mouths do much to ease the transition from outside to inside, the experience afforded by the interior of the tunnels is quite austere and harsh, especially in such sudden contrast to the Swiss landscape through which the roadway passes. It is the aim of the Geneva By-Pass project to develop a treatment of the tunnel interiors that would mitigate their austerity by softening their visual/audio noise levels while enhancing the traveller's kinesthetic experience. Light and sound are perfect media for such a situation because

they do not introduce any barriers or other impediments to one's drive along the road. Presently it is technologically impossible to produce actual Silence with "anti-noise" wave forms, and that is NOT the objective. Instead, this is a proposal to use the vehicular noise trapped in the tunnel as a "raw material" in order to make kinesthetic sense of the driver's underground passage, to re-qualify that huge noise, and to make acoustical "sound fields" from the traffic noise. The Geneva By-Pass seeks to improve the conditions of the way we live by changing qualities of our "surround," not only aesthetically but also physically, actually altering and improving the environment we've made for ourselves. The perceptual quality of the tunnel is the result of the dynamic behavior of sound when restricted by confined space. It is important to understand, however, that the acoustic volume of the tunnel is not simply a matter of cubic measurements. Each cavity has its own modes of sympathetic vibration that must be measured in terms of time, not in spatial dimensions.

Geneva By-Pass has been developed by a relationship of the time of the sound to the time of the tunnel. The behavior of the acoustic cavities, indoors or out, needs to be understood in terms of time and time envelopes. Whether the particular result is made by simple phasing of cycles, or the phasing of intervals, or

ter of architecture. The Geneva By-Pass project is essentially sound architecture by propelling attention from one boundary of the space to the next. The viewer is obligated to move through the linear space in order to

the phasing of events, each and every work relies upon the match or coincidence of the active time of the sound with the passive time of the tunnel. The peripherally confined, frontal nature of sight makes it a perceptual relative of painting, while the 360 degree "scan" of hearing resembles more the three-dimensional charac

integrate what is heard with the strictly visual notions of what space is—the area in, around, or between—while becoming astonishingly aware of a sensibility that deals with light, space, and sound as material, as solid evidence of being.

GENEVA BY-PASS

1.0 Theoretical Vision

Upon entering the tunnel the motorist will first become aware of a single fifty-centimeter-wide band of continuous lights chasing down the length of each tunnel at a rate equal to the speed limit. (The rate of the "chase" would be adjustable by manual override to suit overall traffic conditions.) The driver would also notice that the car had become enveloped in an omnipresent slowly cycling, purring hum, like that of a two-propeller aircraft or a finely tuned road machine. This steady, soothing sound will be penetrated by the sound of the "slipstream," a nearly "white" noise whose sound content or "color" would never be quite the same because it would be adjusted to the varying vehicular content in the tunnel. Influenced by the speed of the moving lights, the motorist would steer the vehicle through an invisible but fluid field of sound that would "cushion" the experience through the tunnel. The travellers would not be aware of the fact that the

presence of the "white" noise was actually reducing the sound pressure level inside the tunnels. This would be a subliminal result, but it should contribute considerably to stress reduction for the drivers. Two types of sound effects will be generated within the tunnel. The first would be a "standing tone," a steady and all-pervasive, masking group of tones that would "qualify" each tunnel. The purr in one tunnel would become the warble found in the next, while the third might be dominated by a prevalent pulse. The second mode of sound treatment involves the use of experimental technology called ACTIVE Noise CONTROL, which has recently been developed for use in reducing the noise level in air-conditioning ducts and industrial exhaust stacks. Considerable research and development work is needed since the ACTIVE Noise CONTROL is still a nascent technology. In this theoretical version, the lighting in the tunnel would be keyed to an external environmental sensor. The layout of the fixtures inside the tunnels would be changed to eliminate the flicker in the driver's peripheral vision imposed by the present intermittent "skip" lighting layout. This band of chasing colored light is responsive to external conditions and linked

MICHAEL BREWSTER

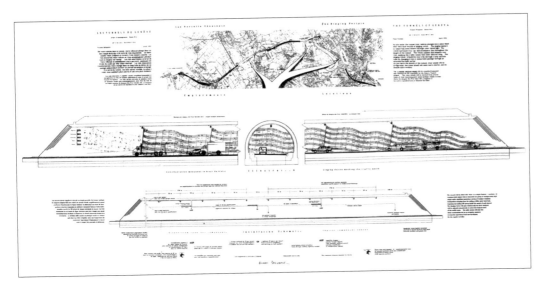

to the overhead traffic signal lights. If a red light-stop emergency condition exists inside one of the tunnels, the chase will stop with all fixtures lit, in a full white-light, stationary mode. Ideally, the lighting system will work as a subliminal traffic regulator. At proper speed, if you entered in a lighted zone, the zone would travel with you through the tunnel; your vehicle always staying within the light. Consequently all sequences of events—the passive sound mask, the active sound mask, and the light chase—will occur at a rate equal to the speed limit, thereby acting as a subliminal guide to all the drivers traversing these subterranean spaces.

2.0 Practical Vision

ACTIVE Noise CONTROL was tested in tunnels in Los Angeles and San Francisco with great success. The technology was then taken to the Geneva By-Pass, but due to the greater length of the tunnels, an untenable number of control devices were needed to successfully reduce the noise level. Research continues with this technology to produce a viable solution for this site. In the practical version, now under construction,* externally pro-duced tones coexist and interact with vocal tones derived from several types of unac-companied music similar in character to music by Josquin des Prez.

The tunnels will be filled with voices in a simple fashion: a multiple CD player will be connected to a group of constant duty high output audio-amplifiers powering a string of weather-resistant loudspeakers hanging from the ceiling at fifty-meter intervals, beginning and ending one hundred meters inside the mouth of each tunnel. The singing voices will play continuously, but their loudness

GENEVA BY-PASS

will be adjusted automatically to match the loudness level of the traffic noises. The audio system will play the music, but in an irregular sequence to keep the experience fresh and developing for the regular traveller. In the Geneva By-Pass, the user behaves sculpturally, probing the sound field as a "Moving Viewer," in this case driving at seventy mph through instead of around volumes, apprehending physical conditions and spatial percepts as unique as thick or thin and active or inactive space. Acoustics itself becomes a perceptual field. The Geneva By-Pass has examined, exposed, and enlarged our understanding of sound as a means for producing an art of spatial percepts free of encumbering artifacts.

*As a result of the 1994 elections, this project, after an extensive competition process and research on the specific acoustics of the site, was terminated.

instrument as architecture

in ' stru . ment [L. *instrumentum*, a tool, implement, stock in trade, furniture, dress, from *instruere*, to furnish, equip; *in*, in, and *struere*, to pile up, arrange.] a mechanical device or tool, such as a surgeon's instrument; a formal legal document; an electronic measuring device, such as a navigator's instrument; a person or a thing used by another for some private end; and any device producing musical sound, as a violin, oboe, or drum.

The following projects deal with structure itself as instrument, or metaphor for instrument. They bring into question and explore the roles of audience, performer, and composer, the interaction between the three roles, and their interaction with the instrument (or tool) itself. In this sense music loses some of its definition as purely vocal or instrumental sound and becomes more closely integrated into a multimedia approach. Because there are no musicians, no composers, no audience, the viewer becomes all these roles. Though we can survey a container from its outside, our sense of its space must develop from its inside, resulting in a complete experience both internally and externally.

Further, there is an inside within the inside of the space—our bodies. Developing an understanding of the ear as a finely tuned instrument for measuring can enhance our perceptions of space. We hear not just with our ears, but with our entire bodies; low frequencies can be heard in the pit of the stomach, just as high frequencies, such as fingernails scratching across a chalkboard, can make the skin crawl. These works attempt to pinpoint the transition between the physical feeling of a space, or architecture, and the emotional feeling of a space, or music. The result is neither purely musical nor architectural, but a hybrid that falls between the two disciplines.

DENARI
FULLMAN
ZEUG DESIGN

CP8706 EXPLODING SONIC TEST— AUDIO VISUAL BIG GUITAR

N E I L D E N A R I

1.0 The composer Glenn Branca has stated that the electric guitar is "just a piece of wood with a microphone on it." Something so simple, yet so powerful: an unlimited machine. Through this openness, the electric guitar is, indeed, the ultimate accessible and controllable American (noise) machine. For forty years it has fulfilled the promise that volume, amplification, and sonic power are inevitable and inescapable culturally expressive responses to our present condition. As with any invention, the device was created to fill a need, a need that still exists. Since its inception, the electric guitar fulfills the definition of its own purpose—it is a musical device, while at the same time, the electric guitar has a cultural relevance beyond its use as a musical instrument. The popular American iconographic image of the electric guitar, created by the histrionic playing of its heroes such as Jimi Hendrix (almost everyone knows he played a right-handed Stratocaster upside down), reinforces the subversive meaning of this guitar device. In fact, the guitar does not even have to be plugged-in or present to be a signifier of our time as any rock-and-roll poster illustrates. These images are so casual, almost subliminal, that we often do not recognize a relentless hegemonic force pulling culture into new, perhaps post-anarchistic, areas. In this, the electric guitar may be seen as a kind of paradigmatic instrument: where the technology of the gui-

tar has remained basically the same, it has nonetheless been an important tool in the construction of cultural evolvement.

Like any potent machine, performance and beauty is virtually indistinguishable in the electric guitar: seeing and hearing is often one and the same.

2.0 Separated from culture, however, the guitar is an instrument of physical laws. The big guitar is a spatial/interactive piece that explores simultaneously the roots of the guitar culturally as well as its physicality. The big guitar is a large aluminum resonator box that the player occupies. It is the scale of the body, between the size of the guitar and a room. Upon entering, the viewer faces the neck, six 10'-0" long strings supported by a fret board and an oscilloscope at el. 5'-2 1/2". Any space is automatically an acoustical container of sounds, the theater or symphony hall being the most specialized in shape. Any change of that space's size and shape effects what we hear. The big guitar uses an interactive rotating roof flap that alters the small space in which the player is

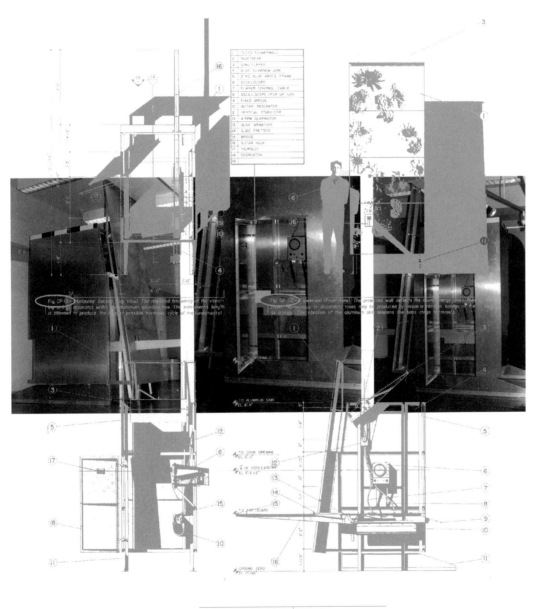

AUDIO VISUAL BIG GUITAR

Audio Visual Big Guitar was constructed in late August 1987 at Columbia University by Mark Brearley, Peter Cook, Larry Daves, Neil Denari, Diana Thater, and Hishman Youssef.

N

E

I

L

D

E

N

A

R

B

I

enclosed. The fixed edges of the space are designed to reflect sound down to the player generating unpredictable geometrical reverberation patterns. Volume, tone, and roof controls may be operated while viewing the sine curve display of the oscilloscope—the visual representation of the frequencies generated by setting the strings into vibratory motion.

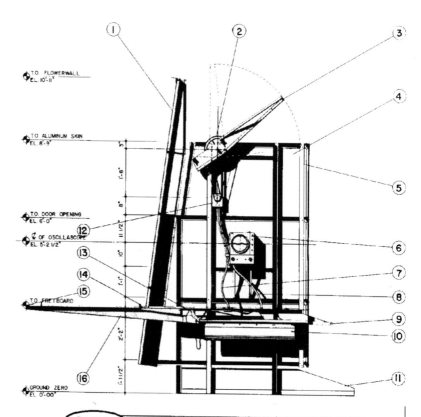

Fig. GP-04—Vertical Section. The signal is then heard through amplification and seen as the oscilliscope produces the sine curve in response to the frequency of the signal. The sound curve of a musical sound Is periodic, it recurs at perfectly regular intervals. It is essentially a graphic display of the actual vibrating string with the waves traveling along its length.

The instrument produces the sound; the player manipulates the sound; and the oscilloscope gives the visual representation of the music in analogue form. The viewer is intrigued in a different and active way with musical exploration, in contrast to the physically passive listening posture of a concert-goer. Though motivated by cultural rebellion, the function of the electric guitar is changing; in harnessing volumetric power it becomes a tool to understand sound itself. Sound can be reduced to an elemental mathematical equation. Mathematics are symbolic of basic structural and conceptual forms. This reflection of mathematics as music refers to the possible monism of mathematics. Martin Heidegger has asserted it to be the "fundamental pre-supposition of all things." By being an instrument of sonic manipulation, architecture joins the ranks of those disciplines involved in a (hopeful) demonstration of a singular language.

AUDIO VISUAL BIG GUITAR

SONIC
SPACE
OF THE
LONG-STRINGED INSTRUMENT

Inside an old candy factory in Austin, black draped walls optically recede, creating the illusion of endless space. One hundred and twenty long strings suspended at waist height define the horizon line. Illuminated from above, the highlights seem to float infinitely in space before dissolving into the void. The Long-Stringed Instrument, a spatial and temporal exploration, evolved over a period of twelve years. Created and refined as a collaboration with engineers and instrument builders experimenting with wire, resonator boxes, and tuning systems, the Long-Stringed Instrument now fills an entire warehouse space.

Physically vast, the strings span eighty-five feet. A performer must enter the installation and move among the wires to make music. Stepping back one becomes a viewer, seeing other players slowly glide through space, in relationship to other performers travelling. Loud sonic textures fill the room; inside the instrument, you are inside the sound.

The music expresses the properties of longitudinally vibrating elongated strings. As the performer's position within the strings continually changes, so do the proportionate lengths created by pressed fingers dampening the strings. The constantly changing lengths produce cascading secondary pitches—the overtones.

These overtones emerge as a matrix of higher pitched harmonic relationships above the notated pitches. Overtones result from the fact that a body vibrates in section as well as along its total length. By focusing on the overtones while slowly walking and rubbing

fingers on wire, the performer experiences the order of nature through the physics of sound. The tone quality produced by the instrument can be described as similar to a bowed cello, but reedier. Multiple parts played at full volume produce the drama of a booming pipe organ. Vibrations, the physical manifestation of sound, move through the body. The shifting of one's attention between the fundamen-

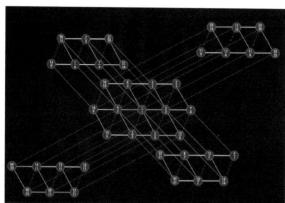

tal pitches and the always changing overtones induces a hyper-meditative state, altering one's perception of time. The intellectual space of harmonic intervals is planar. Stretched harmony, introduced by composer James McCartney, straddles different planes. One moves among these planes in chordal progressions, subjectively twisting space. Dissonance doesn't exist in this system—only added complexity.

Tuning is the matching of a tone on one instrument with the same tone on another instrument by changing the length or tension of a string. Once one tone is matched or tuned on an instrument, all other tones of that instrument can be adjusted to the matched tone. The Long-Stringed Instrument is tuned using a small number proportionate relationship, paralleling the visual world of architecture. The simplest and most harmonic relationship is the octave, 2:1. The next most harmonic is the perfect fifth, 3:2. Other proportional relationships that can be used include 4:3, 5:4, 6:5, and so on. These relationships can be mapped visually,

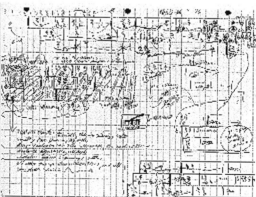

ELLEN f ULLMAN

producing a diagram like
a molecular structure.
The musical notation
for this instrument
evolved alongside the
evolution of the in-
strument itself. A basic
premise of the nota-
tion is that time is
described by distance
walked. At metric intervals, numbered lines
on the floor are used to direct performers
how far to walk. The performers' movements
and the corresponding harmonic transitions
can be coordinated to occur in various relationships to each other: multiple parts staged
in unison, staggered randomly or in symmet-
rical proportions. As the need for musical
sophistication increases, new layers of information are developed into visual symbols and
added to the existing notational form.
Experiencing sound from within the Long-
Stringed Instrument allows us, as audience and
performer, to explore the relationship between
space, time, and sound, to experience the order of nature through the physics of sound.[1]

[1] Influences for the Long-Stringed Instrument are from the work of:
Maryanne Amacher and Phill Niblock—the concept of loud sonic textures,
experienced viscerally; Pauline Oliveros—the concept of performer as observ-
er and the concept of transforming yourself with your work; James Tenny—
the concept of the intellectual space of harmonic intervals.

LONG-STRINGED INSTRUMENT

FREEWAY AS INSTRUMENT

THESE DIAMONDS ON MY WINDSHIELD

ARE THESE TEARS FROM HEAVEN.

I'M PULLING INTO TOWN ON THE INTERSTATE.

I GOT ME A STEEL TRAIN IN THE RAIN

AND THE WIND BITES MY CHEEK THROUGH THE WING.

THIS LATE NIGHT FREEWAY FLYING

ALWAYS MAKES ME SING

IT ALWAYS MAKES ME SING.

Tom Waits
Diamonds On My
Windshield

Music is an inseparable part of the culture of driving. To drive, particularly on the freeway, means to listen to the radio—albums and driving songs. The temporal structure of music seems particularly sympathetic to the experiences of high speed automobile travel, and the rhythm of the road plays impromptu harmonies with the songs blaring out of our speakers. This is a project about music and the road, not only as a celebration of their special relationship in popular culture, but in recognition of the fact that the primary experience in freeway driving is temporal rather that spatial. Traditionally, music is defined as aural elements expressed through time. Freeway as Instrument explores the idea of music as defined by visual elements expressed through time, specifically, shadows cast as the sun traverses the sky, a visual representation of a temporal experience—the cycle of the day. Freeway as Instrument explores the idea that the road itself is an orchestra and the ever-changing and continual shadows that fall across it and beside it are music experienced by drivers and their passengers. In this context, the sun is the conductor, light are the musicians, roadside elements (vegetative and built) are the instruments, and the shadows they cast are the music.

The American city has lost its definitive status as a physical location, challenged by a variety of phenomena that often occur around major nodes of infrastructure or communication. The suburban

sprawl of cities continues with the endless addition of cookie-cutter homes, industrial parks, and the countless mini-malls all interconnected by a network of freeways as a result of nineteenth-century expansion and twentieth-century zoning. This can be said about Houston, Texas, where this project was commissioned and partially constructed by the State Department of Highways.

There is a feeling of sameness on the arrival and departure on the urban freeway system. The overwhelming pressure directed to find favorable locations reinforces this momentum. To make an artistic impact within the endless sequence of exits and entrances, to particularize one interchange and make it unique, to briefly elevate the experience of the freeway to an archetypal realm, one does not look at the

visual or plastic arts for a spatial solution, but rather to the evanescence of music for a temporal one. The forms of the physical elements, either vegetative or built, operate as instruments based solely on the physical properties necessary to create the temporal experience of music. These elements are specifically not intended as art in the sense of plastic or sculptural art, but are choreographed to cast a shadow

FREEWAY AS INSTRUMENT

The development of the submission was a collaboration between Zeug Design, Inc. (John Brown, principle, Joanne Heinen, Eileen Stan, Michael Knudsen, William Semple, Loraine Dearstyne Fowlow, project team) and Mark Hults as consultants to the Texas State Department of Highways.

Z

E

U

G

D

E

S

I

G

N

with a specific shape as well as height, that will play throughout the day. 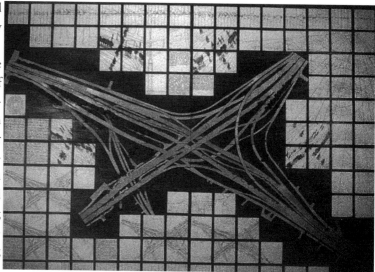 The physical elements, the instruments, composed of vegetation and built elements are not works of art in the sculptural sense. Their form is based solely on creating the necessary condition from which the temporal art of music can spring forth when played by a talented musician following a predetermined score.

As musicians wait in anxious trepidation while the conductor takes the podium, the freeway awaits the dawn, and as the sun peeks over the horizon, the conductor raises the baton and the interchange is filled with the ephemeral rhythms, harmonies, melodies, and counterpoints of the shadow patterns created by the instruments as they are played, their latent potential is realized through the movement of the sun. The quality of light in Texas, where this project is built, engenders the composition with a virtuosity of performance that clarifies the special but often overlooked quality that light brings to this landscape. The daily performance, ranging from pianissimo to fortissimo according to variations in the weather and time of day, renders explicit the subtle, ever-shifting qualities of the environment that are normally lost

within the air-conditioned world of either our buildings or automobiles.

The first instrument is comprised of rows of evergreen trees and, playing the role of a cello in a string quartet, sets the base temporal structure for the piece. The second instrument, analogous to the viola and consisting of a series of masts attached to the roadside, adds harmonic overlays. The third instrument is comprised of deciduous trees of various heights, shapes, and flowering patterns and, playing the role of the first violin, sets the primary melody. The final instrument, consisting of wavelike forms suspended over the road surface, is analogous to the second violin, and shares melodic lead with the first.

Each day brings a cyclical performance of the same general characteristics and solar variations in azimuth and altitude throughout the year adding subtle shifts in tone and harmony. Vegetation growth, leafing cycles, and the four planting/culling plans develop variations on the original theme. The result is a piece whose structure is time dependent, with each performance being subtly unique and tied inseparably to the ever-shifting moods of its location in south central Texas.

FREEWAY AS INSTRUMENT

Layered Relationships

lay'er *a thickness of some material laid on, over or under a surface; a stratum; a bed; etc.*

The following projects deal with a synthesis of layering. Each of the works were designed using a series of independent layers, superimposed together to create a coherent, more inclusive whole. The multiplicity of information addressing movement, language, structure, light, proportion, building technology, site, and spatial arrangement were extracted and analyzed. This is a process that studies the inherent nature of architecture as a multi-layered discipline by combining the constituent elements of separate material into a single unified entity. The resultant overlapping of ideas and layering, juxtapositions and superimpositions, purposefully blurs the standard relationship between graphic conventions of building as plan, section, and elevation and their meanings in the built realm. In these instances, music is one of the several layers of information—*a layer of opportunity.*

HOLL

STUDIOWORKS

NOVAK

STRETTO HOUSE

S

T

E

V

E

N

H

O

L

L

The analogies made between music and architecture have historically generated an overwrought territory of comparisons along narrow channels of interaction: number, rhythm, notation, and proportion. A transference of essential properties or ideas from one art to another could occur through channels not primary to either. In order to look further into transposition along other lines, we could think of architecture and music as unknowns and solve an equation for two unknowns. Where music has a materiality in instrumentation and sound, architecture attempts an analogue in space and light.

$$\frac{material \times sound}{time} = \frac{material \times light}{space}$$

The question would not simply be "how to compare?" but what unmarked routes to investigate and what experiments to perform.

The Stretto House was designed as a parallel to Béla Bartók's *Music for Strings, Percussion and Celestra* (1936). Sited adjacent to three ponds with existing concrete dams, the Stretto House projects the character of the site in a series of concrete block "spatial dams" with metal-framed "aqueous space" flowing through them. Coursing over the dams, like the overlapping Stretto[*] in music, water is an overlapping reflection of the landscape outside as well as the virtual overlapping of the space inside.

Bartók's use of folk music, which he collected as material for his work, and his mathematical approach to and

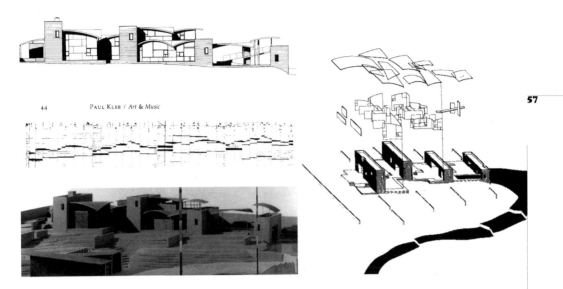

PAUL KLEE / *Art & Music*

44

manipulation of this material are the raw materials that determine the details of the music. In music as well as in architecture, form, rhythm, proportion, and mathematics are of elementary importance. Speaking of this Bartók wrote: "We are concerned not only with achievements of purely scientific issues, but also those which have a stimulating effect on composers. According to the natural order of things, practice comes theory." In architecture we are also concerned with a process that stimulates the result. The Hungarian musicologist, Erno Lendvai, pointed out there is an evident *mismatch* that coexists between Bartók's highly personalized expression and his systematic compositional technique. This multi-layered combination of mismatches can be seen in the resulting direct representation of experience in both the music and the house.

Bartók's composition is in four movements and has a distinct division in materiality between heavy (percussion) and light (strings). The Stretto House is formed in four sections, each consisting of two modes: heavy orthogonal masonry and light, curvilinear metal (the concrete block and metal structures of Texas vernacular). The plan is purely orthogonal; the section, curvilinear. The guest house is an inversion with the plan curvilinear and section orthogonal, similar to the inversions of the subject in the first movement of Bartók's score. The spatial relationship created from the rectangular contrasted with the curvilinear becomes a *mismatch* that results from the meeting of the golden mean with the curve. In the main house aqueous space is developed by several means: floor plans pull the level of one space through to the next, roof planes pull space over walls, and an arched wall pulls light down from a skylight.

STRETTO HOUSE

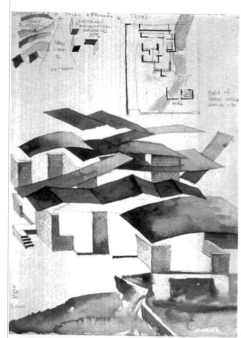

In both works, the music and the house, you are left with the sense that something remains hidden, that several layers are at work beneath the structure. For example, Bartók's fugue in the first movement consists in its entirety of 89 bars, while the number of bars in each section of the movement clearly approximates the Fibonacci sequence. The Fibonacci numbers are the unending sequence 1, 2, 3, 5, 8, 13, 21, 34, etc. where each term is defined as the sum of its two predecessors or $a:b = a + b, a<b$. One senses the intentions of Bartók's music from the manner in which all the major turning points in the first movement are related to this sequence: the strings remove their mutes in bar 34; a climax is reached in bar 56; the celestra appears on the upbeat in bar 77. There results a multi-layered combination of *mismatches* as befits the Fibonacci sequence to which Bartók is thought to have recourse. This layering of *mismatches,* which Bartók uses as a tool to compose his music, is then applied to architecture and is the raw material that determines the resulting details of the house.

The Fibonacci sequence's method of dividing and organizing natural numbers is similar to that present in the Golden Section. The Golden Section is the proportion of the two divisions of a straight line such that the smaller is to the sum of the two. Suggesting the possibility of comparable methods of study, the Stretto House uses Golden Section relationships throughout expressed by: solid/void relationships of walls and

gesting thought and development open up. The correspondence across these once separated territories may not follow purely "reasonable" lines. Two children from totally different cultures, lacking a shared language, could meet and "interact" by means other than verbal correspondence. Collapsed boundaries open crossroads and galleries of connection—opportunities to establish a more direct architecture in the dynamic condition of twentieth-century culture. Analyzing music as an approach to architecture is only one way of confronting pressures toward autonomy of architecture, or its validation by historical precedent alone. A move away from compartmentalizing and mental closing is a move toward an open future.

openings, window mullions, mirrors, cabinets, and drawers. Between the four bars floats a contrasting system: wavelike roof forms and curved cast glass fill in the space between the rectangular and the curve. Almost every surface has a trace of the Golden Section overlaid with a second set of curved references. The spatial relationship created from the rectangular contrasted with the curvilinear becomes a *mismatch*. Since the aqueous spaces remain through the medium of the *mismatches*, there also results a multi-layered combination of *mismatches* similar to that used by Bartók. As boundaries between disciplines collapse, new channels sug-

*Stretto in music is applied to the entrances of compositional themes, usually in fugal works, where the different voices do not wait for each other to finish stating the fugal subject but pile in on top of each other. It is important not to confuse the polyphonic form of a cannon with the device of the stretto. In a cannon the imitation is continuous, preserving a fair distance between voices, while in a stretto it is momentary and accelerated—occurring in rapid succession. The result is an allusion of concentration of musical matter and an accelerating clash of musical events.

Klaus Liepmann. *The Language of Music.* New York: The Ronald Press Company, p. 275.

STRETTO HOUSE

GRAND CENTER—ST. LOUIS

Studioworks: Robert Mangurian and Mary-Ann Ray with Mary Miss and James Turrell
Technical Consultant: Kent Hodgetts, Music Consultant: Eugene Kupper

This master plan for the Grand Center Arts and Entertainment District of St. Louis is based on a set of underlying physical, functional, and conceptual principles. These principles are the foundation for the plan evolution and configuration, and are formalized as seven compositional strategies—the seven layers. The richness and complexity of the district as it is and the program that emerges from the strategies are incorporated into the master plan. The seven layers evolved after studying the area and discovering nuances where elements could intercede to have the most effect on transforming the area. The aim was to use what was there and strengthen it within the master plan. Each layer has a piece of music dedicated to it, which explains the character of the layer.

Grand Center is realized as overlapping systems that all operate at the same time, similar to the relationship of each instrument's part to a music score. The word "score" comes from the name given to the process of drawing vertical lines through the music. The notes of each instrument's part are spaced in such a way that all sounds meant to be heard together are lined up. Scoring is similar to a surveyor's practice of "marking off" the land. Plans for Grand Center were "marked off" much like a conductor would mark off his score. The conductor of an orchestra must thoroughly analyze the parts of the score before coming to an understanding of it as a whole—as a synthesis of the individual parts. The same is true with analyzing the city and the approach to the master plan of Grand Center.

The objective is to analyze Grand Center to reveal its specific structure and elements, its nature as a city; and to develop a process of decision making in which the design is created directly from given suppositions and then combines what is found into a unified entity. It is hoped that this non-singular and layered method of design will lead to a master plan capable of fulfilling the full range of experiences existing in the life of our cities as we enter into the twenty-first century.

SEVEN LAYERS

Each of the seven layers contains its own functions, creates its own form, and radiates its own state of mind. The layers are put together in a well-defined system of physical, social, and aesthetic ideas in an urban district. The urban context and program determine the organization of the seven layers. Each layer makes a strong proposal for at least one architectonic aspect. The characteristic of each layer is sharply defined; together, these characteristics communicate the essence of the project.

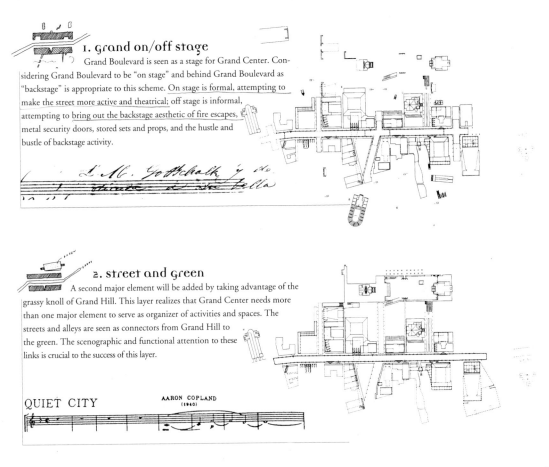

1. Grand on/off stage

Grand Boulevard is seen as a stage for Grand Center. Considering Grand Boulevard to be "on stage" and behind Grand Boulevard as "backstage" is appropriate to this scheme. On stage is formal, attempting to make the street more active and theatrical; off stage is informal, attempting to bring out the backstage aesthetic of fire escapes, metal security doors, stored sets and props, and the hustle and bustle of backstage activity.

2. street and green

A second major element will be added by taking advantage of the grassy knoll of Grand Hill. This layer realizes that Grand Center needs more than one major element to serve as organizer of activities and spaces. The streets and alleys are seen as connectors from Grand Hill to the green. The scenographic and functional attention to these links is crucial to the success of this layer.

QUIET CITY

AARON COPLAND
(1940)

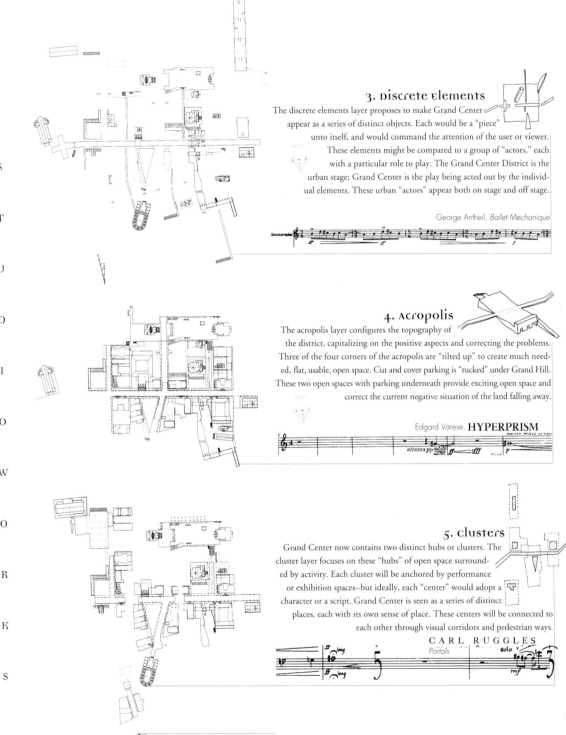

3. discrete elements

The discrete elements layer proposes to make Grand Center appear as a series of distinct objects. Each would be a "piece" unto itself, and would command the attention of the user or viewer. These elements might be compared to a group of "actors," each with a particular role to play. The Grand Center District is the urban stage; Grand Center is the play being acted out by the individual elements. These urban "actors" appear both on stage and off stage.

George Antheil, Ballet Mechanique

4. acropolis

The acropolis layer configures the topography of the district, capitalizing on the positive aspects and correcting the problems. Three of the four corners of the acropolis are "tilted up" to create much needed, flat, usable, open space. Cut and cover parking is "tucked" under Grand Hill. These two open spaces with parking underneath provide exciting open space and correct the current negative situation of the land falling away.

Edgard Varese, **HYPERPRISM**

5. clusters

Grand Center now contains two distinct hubs or clusters. The cluster layer focuses on these "hubs" of open space surrounded by activity. Each cluster will be anchored by performance or exhibition spaces–but ideally, each "center" would adopt a character or a script. Grand Center is seen as a series of distinct places, each with its own sense of place. These centers will be connected to each other through visual corridors and pedestrian ways.

CARL RUGGLES
Portals

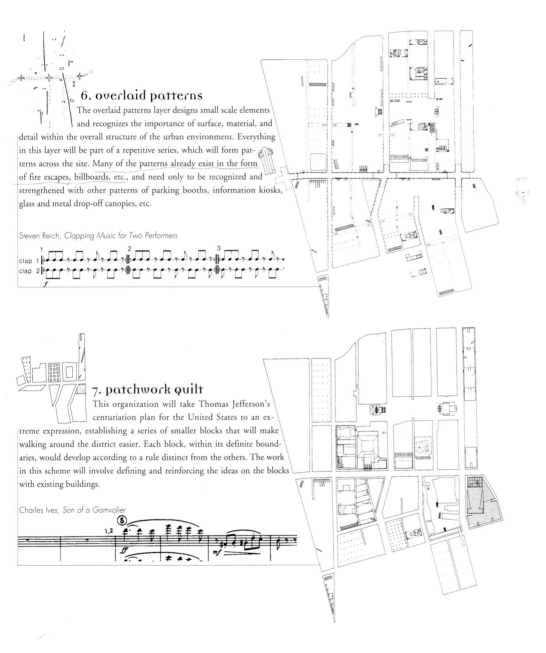

6. overlaid patterns

The overlaid patterns layer designs small scale elements and recognizes the importance of surface, material, and detail within the overall structure of the urban environment. Everything in this layer will be part of a repetitive series, which will form patterns across the site. Many of the patterns already exist in the form of fire escapes, billboards, etc., and need only to be recognized and strengthened with other patterns of parking booths, information kiosks, glass and metal drop-off canopies, etc.

Steven Reich, *Clapping Music for Two Performers*

7. patchwork quilt

This organization will take Thomas Jefferson's centuriation plan for the United States to an extreme expression, establishing a series of smaller blocks that will make walking around the district easier. Each block, within its definite boundaries, would develop according to a rule distinct from the others. The work in this scheme will involve defining and reinforcing the ideas on the blocks with existing buildings.

Charles Ives, *Son of a Gamvolier*

GRAND CENTER—ST. LOUIS

COMPUTATION AND COMPOSITION

jargon: L-system sketches are used as forms determined by isosurfaces taken through number fields.

It all depends on what you believe: Is music an expression of an idea or feeling, or is it an outcome of an exploration into certain relationships in temporal, aural, visual, or other spaces? Chiasmus: Don't we explore the expressions of ideas and feelings and express ourselves in explorations?

Aristid Lindenmeyer: "The essential differences between Chomsky grammars and L-systems lies in the method of applying productions. In Chomsky grammars productions are applied sequentially, whereas in L-systems they are applied in parallel and simultaneously replace all the letters in a given word. This difference reflects the biological motivations of L-systems."

We stand at the dawn of an era that will see the emancipation of architecture from matter. The intuition that allows us to even consider architecture as "frozen music" or music as "molten architecture"

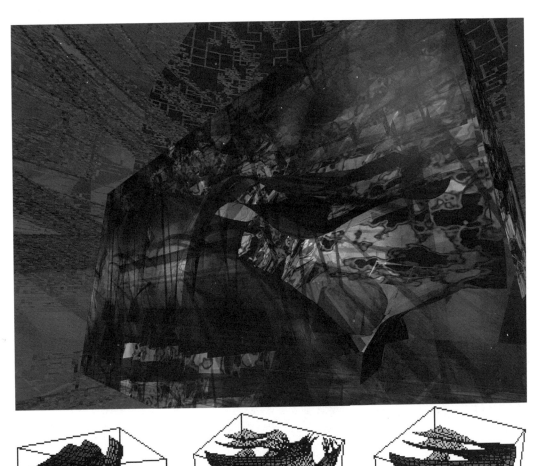

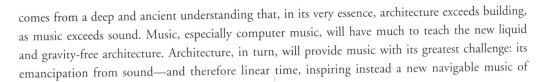

COMPUTATION AND COMPOSITION

comes from a deep and ancient understanding that, in its very essence, architecture exceeds building, as music exceeds sound. Music, especially computer music, will have much to teach the new liquid and gravity-free architecture. Architecture, in turn, will provide music with its greatest challenge: its emancipation from sound—and therefore linear time, inspiring instead a new navigable music of

M

A

B

C

O

S

N

O

V

A

K

places. Together, architecture and music will stand as the arts closest to the functioning of the human cognitive and affective apparatus. The computer will act as the bridge allowing us to truly enter the intimate structures of the two arts for the first time. In dataworlds, buildings flow and music is inhabited. Architecture and music are bonded into a new discipline: archimusic.

How is an archimusic created within a dataworld? Within the computer's memory resides a digitized microcosm of images, sounds, and symbols, whose organization intersects with that inherent in the machine's structure, forming new dynamic interference patterns. Two- and three-dimensional matrices of numbers are created in one of three ways: by computation, by scanning and sampling, or by direct input. These numbers occupy space with qualities that form a "potential archimusic." The same underlying set of numbers—or, in more advanced compositions, functions—can serve as sources for numerous works. Three dimensional contours through these fields of numbers form continuous or discontinuous surfaces that can be traversed in various ways. Each trajectory is different

and the "experience" of travelling through it depends both on the inherent geometry of the surface and on the temporal manner in which it is traversed: the outcome of rapid motion differs from the outcome of slow or intermittent motion.

The surfaces produced this way are not treated as final form; that is to say, they are not understood as constituting the appearance of the work. Rather, they are seen as variations in parameter space that affect the perceivable object indirectly, by controlling the behavior of its visible, audible, or otherwise sensible attributes. Once parameter surfaces are generated, various algorithms are used to extract layers of information in various forms: points, lines, planes, solids, clouds, and so on. The logic by which each layer is extracted can differ, and yet, because the variations are controlled by a relatively small set of composed parameter spaces, the results maintain essential elements of the original form. The extracted layers, in turn, become input to other processes that bring them closer to the desired final form, whether it is sound, color, form, movement, or some combination of these and other end effects.

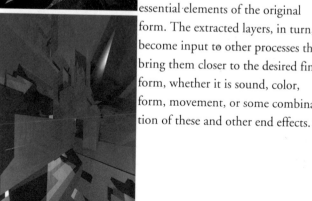

The subcomponents that result from this process are then taken to be operands to a final set of operations. The operations can be the familiar one of addition, subtraction, and so on, or can be invented for the purpose at hand. One set of components can then be subtracted from another, for instance, to produce a particular result, while another pair may be added, multiplied, morphed, torqued, and so on.

At any point there is space for both fact and fiction. Constraints can be driven by logical or illogical desires. The underlying systems simply form strange attractors for the eventual, only temporary, final work. To a great extent, what ensures the strength of the work is not so much the utilitarian logic of any of its steps, but the depth of process, the number of qualitatively distinct kinds of operations that the original dataset undergoes.

The literal spatialization of music in cyberspace, along with the liquefaction of architecture, will allow such sensibilities to become more visible and therefore more accessible. The new spaces of sound within a dataworld will revitalize our collective aural and visual imaginations. And from this dataworld we will construct a new architecture and music, an entirely new poetics, for a new place.

COMPUTATION AND COMPOSITION

ARCHITECTURE and MUSIC Any one who attempt to relate architecture and music at the end of the second millennium must first ask: What music? What architecture? The topic of music and architecture is an ancient one, and any attempt to broach the subject that fails to acknowledge and account for the changes that have occurred and are still occurring is sure to be full of unintended but inevitable erroneous resonances. Let me therefore be clear: when I speak of architecture and music, I am not evoking the ghosts of Pythagoras and Palladio, nor am I referring to the ideal, *a priori* order of the "Music of the Spheres," or some kind of facile superficial architectural and musical impressionism or expressionism. I am interested in architecture and music as grounds for the present and poetic processes for the making of the future; especially in those areas that are just now opening to examination. I am not interested in the stable core of the known, but in the turbulent edge of the barely conceivable.

What architecture? What music? While both fields have undergone dramatic changes, and are neither monolithic nor homogeneous, music has reinvented itself in far more profound ways than architecture has dared.

BEYOND PYTHAGORAS Xenakis claims that we are all Pythagoreans. Perhaps this is so, since we are obviously still enamored with numbers. Most of our conceptions about the relationship of architecture to music are remnants of Pythagorean belief. The most prevalent conception is concerned with the static balance of fixed, perfect parts, eternal because desiccated, desiccated because imagined to preexist in an ideal, immaterial world. Music itself has moved, however, leaving those concerns behind. To associate music and architecture in that way is to associate architecture with the corpse of a long-dead musical and cosmological tradition.

In this century alone, we have witnessed a series of emancipations: in Arnold Schönberg, the emancipation of dissonance; in Edgard Varèse, the emancipation of noise; in Iannif Xenakis, the emancipation of stochastic form; in John Cage, the emancipation of nonintention. To speak of architecture and music at this point in the history of music is to issue a demanding challenge to architecture, for it implies that architecture must confront, parallel, and exceed each of those emancipations and be prepared to travel as far from its own conventional definitions as music has traveled in the course of this century. What does it mean to carry architecture through a parallel series of emancipations? What is the architecture of dissonance? The architecture of noise? What is a stochastic architecture or an architecture of nonintention? And if these are the questions that have already been grappled with, what are the questions still to come?

SOUND BUILDING Consider the transformation in our ability to represent a musical event. In terms of discrimination of pitch, we have gone from the tonal to the chromatic scale, from tone to semitone to quarter tone to any fraction of the octave we desire to use for a composition. In terms of discrimination of duration, we have gone from a large fraction of a whole note to one-forty-eight-thousandth of a second (the duration of a single digital sample); in terms of discrimination of intensity, from a few steps of loudness between pianissimo to twenty bit resolution (over a million steps between silence and maximum intensity). These changes have rendered traditional music theory obsolete because it can no longer even address the vast majority of accessible sound. Image processing and computer graphics have brought the same kind of changes to the visual world. The typesetting machine that places the characters of this page can resolve thousands of dots per inch. In three dimensional form, computer-aided manufacturing machines already achieve tolerances of one-five-thousandth of an inch. With the advent of technology of three-dimensional scanning, volume rendering, particle-based prototyping, and advanced computer manufacturing, as well as concurrent advances in material science, form and space have yet to be explored as thoroughly. Conventional architectural theories and practices have little to give in this domain. Like obsolete theories of music, they simply cannot address the currently available range of possibilities, let alone contend with what the future will bring.

BREAKING the CAGE of ARCHITECTURE In 1967, long before architecture began discussing the notion of the fold, Pierre Boulez wrote *Pli Selon Pli*, literally "ply upon ply" or "fold upon fold," folding a poem by Stéphane Mallarmé into a piece of music. Pierre Boulez wrote: "In the poem in question, the words 'pli selon pli' are used by the poet to describe the way in which the mist, as it disperses, gradually reveals the architecture of the city of Bruges." In 1958, John Cage wrote the *Fontana Mix*, whose score consists of independent transparent layers of points, lines, curves, and surfaces rearranged for each performance. Years later, Parc de la Villette was designed using a series of independent layers of points, lines, and surfaces.

In both cases, acoustic and visual, we have an instance of the grain of control over an artifact becoming finer than the grain of the concepts with which such artifacts are discussed. Simply stated, the grain of architecture has become finer than the grain of current architectural theory and practice. In embracing science and technology, music faced and attempted to resolve the problems engendered by this situation long before architecture—all the more reason to try and understand the future of architecture through the present of music.

Today, these explorations continue: from places of instruments to instruments as places, from expressive performance to inspired derivation, from willfulness to nonintention, the projects gathered in this volume demonstrate the continuing fertility of the challenges music and architecture issue one another.

Music has not yet freed itself from the straight and narrow of time, and architecture may have broken the box, but it has yet to break out of its cage.

Marcos Novak, 28 December 1993

the arts are not isolated,

                              froM one another
                                bUt engage in dialogue
                              thiS
                  understanding wIll
                      introduCe

                                          new kinds
                      of spAtial
                  phenomenoN, however each art
                      can Do

                                          what
                          An
                      otheR
                          Cannot
                      it Has been
                      predIctable
                  therefore, thaT
                          nEw
                      musiC will be answered by
                          The new
                  architectUre -
                          woRk we have
                  not yet seEn

                                      - only heard.

to

```
     eLIZabeth! eLIZabeth!


     hopefully Musical
            Architecture
            pRoduces a new sense
       of locaTion
       for thInking
            aNd


        becoMes
          A
       diffeRent place
          That
was always In the air for
someone to Notice

                    like silence.
```

John Cage

PERFERVID DEFINITIONS

MUSIC the opposite of noise. **ARCHITECTURE** men with big egos that give too many hints. **TRANSLATION** ИОITА⅃ꙅИAЯT. **SOUND** when the tree falls in the forest and you're there. **TIME AND SPACE** speed of light. **TEXT** that's in the other PA. **IMAGE** american politics. **TEMPORAL STRUCTURES** deep-fried watches. **PITCH** I in 12 so it drains properly. **CONTROLLED ACCIDENTS** children. **GOLDEN SECTION** and **GOLDEN MEAN** golden handcuffs or the umbilical chord. **MIDDLE GROUND** equally distant from where you are now. **PRISTINE INNOCENCE** indescribable. **REGIME of the ORIGINAL** madonna, et. al. **COMMUNICATION** speed of light. **CONSTRUCTION** megabytes. **FEEDBACK** neil young's ABC; kronos quartet imitating hendrix. **MEANING** jargon of the authentic. **FORM** FROM. **KNOWLEDGE** unqualified to answer. **COMPUTERIZATION** I/rule of thumb. **MOVEMENT** the long scarf gets caught in spokes and the neck snaps. **DENSITY** deep time. **LAYERED PLANES** great discontinuity. **REVERBERATIONS** JFK. **TONES** earth. **LINEARITY** the straight and narrow. **INTERVENTION ARTISTIQUE** listening to prozac. **CYCLICAL** go talk to cicadeas. **IMPROVISATION** physics plus cicciolina. **MINIMAL** less than most things. **CULTURE** refinement that activates the mind. **KULTURE** charming vulgarity that activates the mind (cross the railroad tracks you'll find it). **ACOUSTICAL** a church. **INSTRUMENT** you. **MEMBRANE** tympanic. **DECAY** lack of volume at the end of sound. **COLOR**(s).**STRETTO** a cafe that makes a real cafe americano. **SCALE** truck. **COUNTERPOINT** needlepoint. **GUITAR** lighter fluid (the story of jimi hendrix). **ALGORITHMIC COMPOSITION** navigating music using math as a justification. **CYBERSPACE** sensitive space; boldly go where no man has gone before. **WHITE NOISE** honky noise. **CHROMATICISM** C D E F G A B C becomes C C# D D# E F F# G G# A A# B C. **DIALOGUE** I:900. **INSTALLATION** a temporary setup like a successful blind date. **THEME** park. **FREEWAY** in new jersey there's a .35 toll every ten minutes. **MOTIVE** to make your own opportunity. **ENVELOPE** the right stuff. **SENSORIUM** sex motel @ $60/hr. **STATIC** what your parents give you when you moved out and what you gave them when you lived there; it's important to note that static is cyclical. **NOTE** to make a point. **AUDIBLE** say what? **VISUAL** fountainhead wannabees. **QUADRO HIFI** it's an orgasmatron. **WIRELESS IMAGINATION** nonbroadcast, broadcast. **COLLABORATION** challenging for architects and the most fun for musicians. **BOUNDARY** separates you from the joneses. **INTERFERENCE** football. **SPECTATOR** rear window. **ECHO** the apocalyptic other. **APPARATUS** the wilted gesture. **WARBLE** isn't that a bird? **CAVITY** aim without crest or colgate. **VIBRATION** good. **KINESTHETIC EXPERIENCE** getting jerked-off on a ny subway. **SCAN** appropriation scam. **OSCILLOSCOPE** sometimes they work; sometimes they don't. **AESTETHICISM** it's kind of a personal thang. **PAMPHLET** the alternative PA.

george newburn and peter noble

SUGGESTED READINGS

I. MUSIC AND ARCHITECTURE

Beranek, L. *Music, Acoustics and Architecture.* New York: Wiley & Sons, 1962.

Conrads, Ulrich, editor. "The Audible Space." *Daidalos* 17 (1985).

Sessions, R. *The Experience of Composer, Performer, Listener.* New York: Atheneum, 1962.

Vergani, Gianmarco, editor. "Fragments of Culture." *Precis* 6 (New York: Rizzoli International, 1988).

II. ARCHITECTURE

Bright, Michael. *Cities Built to Music.* Columbus: Ohio State University Press, 1984.

"Le Corbusier's La Tourette." *Architectural Record* 128 (July 1960).

"Harmonics in Architecture." *Abacu* 2 (1980).

III. MUSIC

Attali, Jaques. *Noise: The Political Economy of Music.* Minneapolis: University of Minnesota, 1985.

Cage, J. *A year from Monday.* London: Wesleyan University Press, 1968, p. 14, pp. 36–42.

Dahlhaus, Carl. *The Idea of Absolute Music.* Trans. Roger Lustig. Chicago: University of Chicago Press, 1989.

Johnson, Tom. *The Voice of New Music.* Netherlands: Het Apollohuis, 1989.

Nattiez, Jean-Jacques. *Music and Discourse.* Trans. Carolyn Abbate. Princeton: Princeton University Press, 1990.

Nyman, Michael. *Experimental Music: Cage and Beyond.* New York: Schirmer Books, 1974, pp. 27, 28.

Schnebel, D. *Denkbare Musik.* Keulen: Du Mont-Schauberg, 1972, pp. 76, 77.

Schönberg, A. *Style and Idea.* New York: Philosophical Library, 1950.

IV. SOUND SOURCES

Rayleigh, John. *Theory of Sound.* New York: Dover Publications, 1945.

Reichenbach, H. *The Direction of Time.* Berkeley: University of California Press, 1956.

Winckel, Fritz. *Music, Sound and Sensation.* New York: Dover Publications, 1967.

V. SUPPLEMENT

Barthes, Roland. *Image / Music / Text.* Trans. Stephen Heath. New York: Hill & Wang, 1977.

Boulez, Pierre 1985. *Orientations.* Boston: Harvard University Press, p. 176.

Chomsky, Noam and Morris Halle. *The Sound Pattern of English.* New York: Harper & Row, 1968.

Lindenmeyer, Aristid and Premyslaw Prusinkicwicz. *The Algorithmic Beauty of Plants.* New York: Springer-Verlag, 1990, pp. 2–3.

Kahn, Douglas and Gregory Whitehead, editors. *Wireless Imagination.* Cambridge: MIT Press, 1992.

Marcus, Greil. *Ranters and Crowd Pleasers.* New York: Doubleday, 1993.

Small, C. *Music—Society—Education.* London: John Calder, 1977.

CONTRIBUTORS

Maryanne Amacher lives in Kingston, New York. She studied with Arnold Schönberg and has received many awards and grants, including a three-year fellowship (1973–76) at the Center for Advanced Visual Studies at M.I.T. She was recently the musician-in-residence at Mills College, and is writing a piece for the Kronos Quartet. She has performed throughout this country, Europe, and Japan, at places including Capp Street Project (SF), Exit Art (NY), Paula Copper Gallery (NY), and DAAD Gallery (Berlin).

Michael Brewster resides in Venice, California. He received his MFA in sculpture from Claremont Graduate School. He is now an associate professor of art at Claremont College. He has received four NEA grants and one from the Guggenheim Memorial Foundation. He has exhibited at Galleria del Cavallino (Italy), Whitney Museum of American Art (NY), Art Gallery of New South Wales (Australia), and Musée Art Moderne (Paris), and throughout this country and Europe.

John Brown works in Calgary, Alberta. He teaches at and heads the Department of Architecture at the University of Calgary. He is principle of the firm Zeug Design, Inc.

John Cage has become an institutionally recognized name and his work will live forever.

Neil Denari lives in Los Angeles, California. He received his M.Arch. from Harvard University and shortly thereafter opened his firm, Cortex. He teaches design and drawing at SCI-Arc and has been a visiting critic at University of Texas at Arlington, Architectural Association, and Columbia University. His work has been exhibited throughout this country, Japan, and Europe. Princeton Architectural Press is publishing a forthcoming monograph of his work.

David Arthur Hadlock lives in Long Beach, California. He has an MFA in design from California Institute of the Arts. He is a professor of art at California State University, Long Beach and has designed books for various institutions, including the J. Paul Getty Museum.

Ellen Fullman works in Austin, Texas. Her BFA in sculpture is from the Kansas City Art Institute, and she has received several fellowships including Meet the Composer Consortium Commission. Her CD entitled *Body Music* on label XI was published by The Experimental Intermedia Foundation.

Steven Holl resides in New York, New York. He is a professor of architecture at Columbia University and started his own firm in 1976. He has built works throughout this country and Japan, and has exhibited at the Museum of Modern Art, Walker Art Center, and other various galleries. He began, founded, and continues the *Pamphlet Architecture* series.

Bernhard Leitner lives in Vienna, Austria. He studied architecture in Vienna and is a professor at the Academy of Applied Arts in Vienna. His work has been exhibited throughout the world including at PS 1, Museum Haus Lange, Venice Biennale, and Akademie der Kunste. He has written many articles on architecture for *Artforum, Art in America,* and *Daidalos,* and a book entitled *The Architecture of Ludwig Wittgenstein* (Halifax/London).

Robert Mangurian works in Venice, California. He directs the graduate program at the Southern California Institute of Architecture (SCI-Arc), and is one of the founders of the school. He has been a visiting critic at various architecture schools including University of Virginia and Harvard University. He is principle of the firm Studioworks in California and Atelier Italia in Italy. He received an NEA grant for his research of Hadrian's Villa in Italy. He has lectured and exhibited throughout Europe and the U.S.

Elizabeth Martin lives in Los Angeles, California. She attended the Manhattan School of Music Preparatory School (1972-81) with the support of the Rockefeller Foundation. She also attained a B.Arch. from Tulane University and an M.Arch. from SCI-Arc. Her work has been exhibited at 2AES, Limn, and Hopper House.

George Newburn resides in Los Angeles, California. He has a B.Arch. from SCI-Arc. He has, for several years, taught at Atelier Italia in Italy and is currently teaching acoustics at SCI-Arc. He is a principle of Studio bau: ton, an architecture firm specializing in sound studios, and recently he has been concerned about women's rights in the field of architecture.

Peter Noble works in Los Angeles, California. With a B.Arch. from Cornell University and an M.Arch. from SCI-Arc, he is currently an associate at Hodgetts & Fung and can often be seen mountain-bike riding in Topanga Canyon.

Marcos Novak lives in Austin, Texas. He is a Ph.D. candidate at the University of California at Los Angeles and is an assistant professor of architecture at the University of Texas at Austin. His work has been exhibited at SCI-Arc, New Museum of Contemporary Art in NY, and at various conferences, including Cyberspace 1993.

Maryann Ray works in Venice, California. She has an M.Arch. from Princeton University and is a fellow at the American Academy of Rome. She teaches design and various seminars at SCI-Arc and is a principle in the firm Studioworks in California, as well as Atelier Italia in Italy. Her work has been exhibited at the Gallery of Functional Art, SCI-Arc, and the Los Angeles Municipal Gallery.

Designed by David Arthur Hadlock
Text set in Adobe Garamond,
Democratica, Quartet, and Futura.
photographs by individual
architects, musicians, or artists except
where noted.

The cover of this pamphlet was created as a computer alloy. From each of the case studies a representative of the work—either a sketch, model, drawing or built object—was selected. The basic idea was to layer together an image from each case study to create an integra-ted whole, resulting in a visual fusion or blending of a ten-part counterpoint. These observations and their inherent possibilities were the mental touchstones from which *Pamphlet Architecture 16* evolved.

The structure of the computer alloy uses collage and layering as seen in music—namely the principles of counterpoint. Further, the process is like a tapestry in which the figure and the field shift supporting roles where structure and expression meet. From the teachings of Paul Klee at the Bauhaus, we have learned that a drawing in this contrapuntal manner demonstrates the continuity of spectral color and the movement inherent within the interaction of the shapes.

As part of the procedure, Marcos Novak took several independent images and created visual sound of them. The hearing process is translated into binary mathematics. Then, the imprinted form, which records movements of the sound pattern, is blended within the image. Through this technology the human auditory system is detailed by means of advanced computer technology, thereby translating a musical concept into visual terms. The cover image arrived at a new paradigm of relationships, which is called an alloy.

Both the cover and the content of *PA16* is a collection of works that speak to one another in the present, while looking to a future where every voice has its own part within a coherent whole, like the effect created by a polyphonous chorus—*a harmony of unexpected likeness.*—E.M.